My First Irish World Atlas

Written and designed by
Tony Potter • Dee Costello
Helen Keith • Pat Hegarty
Kevin Knight • Emily Smyth

Edited by **Lisa Regan**

Illustrated by **Jo Moore**

GILL & MACMILLAN

All about maps

CONTENTS

If you are looking for a country, go to page 40 and look under the first letter of the country name, for example Ireland is under the letter 'I'.

A map is a picture of a place seen from above. Imagine what your home would look like if you flew over it in a space rocket and took photographs. It would show the area around your home spread out flat, getting smaller in scale as you move further away.

We've taken a ride in a space rocket so we can learn how maps work. It's amazing how much you can see from up here!

My House

This is a picture of our home from high above, as we took off in the space rocket.

The world

This big map shows you what the world would look like if it were flattened out. The differently coloured areas of land are called continents. There are seven continents and five oceans in the world.

This is planet Earth. Imagine a line around its middle. This is called the Equator.

This book shows you some of the people, animals, plants and places found in each continent.

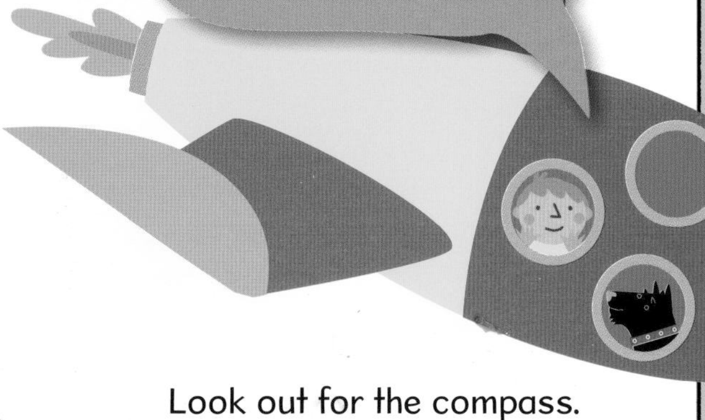

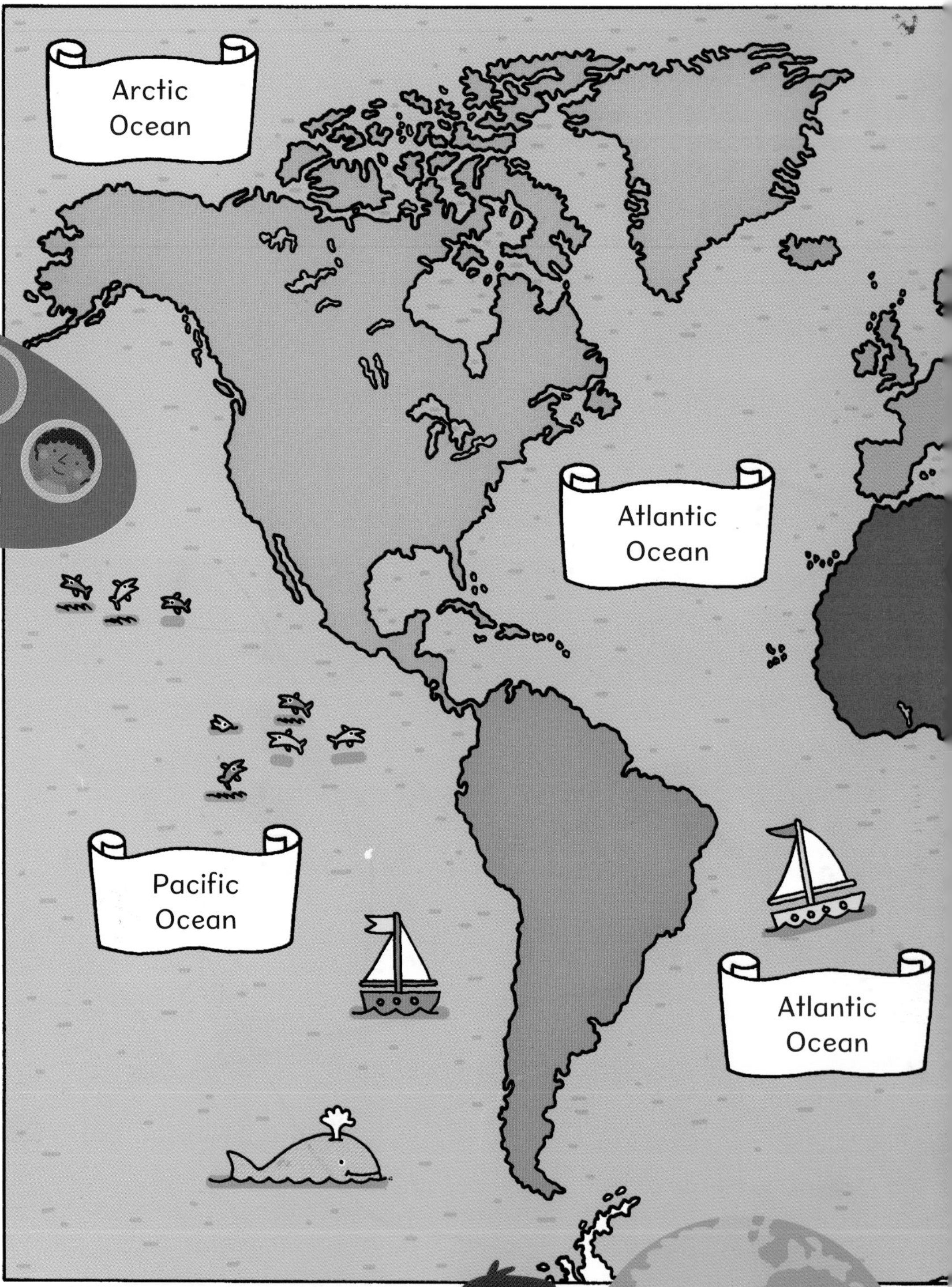

Look out for the compass. The needle points to these directions: N for North, E for East, S for South and W for West.

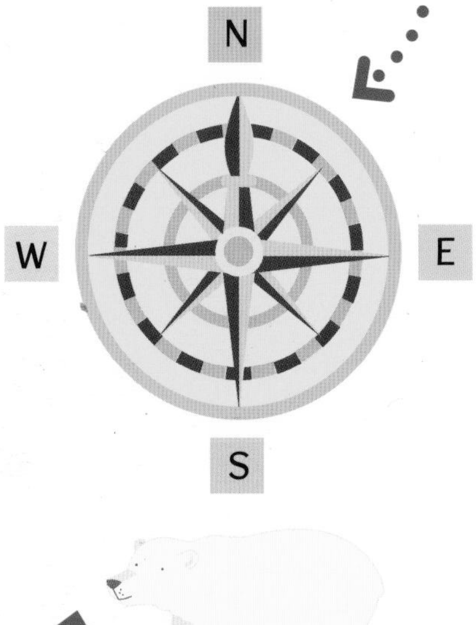

N

W E

S

Polar bears are found at the North Pole, penguins are found at the South Pole.

Arctic Ocean

Atlantic Ocean

Pacific Ocean

Atlantic Ocean

The bottom half of the world is called the Southern Hemisphere.

South Pole

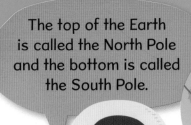

The top of the Earth is called the North Pole and the bottom is called the South Pole.

North Pole

South Pole

The poles are the coldest places on Earth. It is hottest around the Equator.

Look out for this map to see where each country belongs in the world.

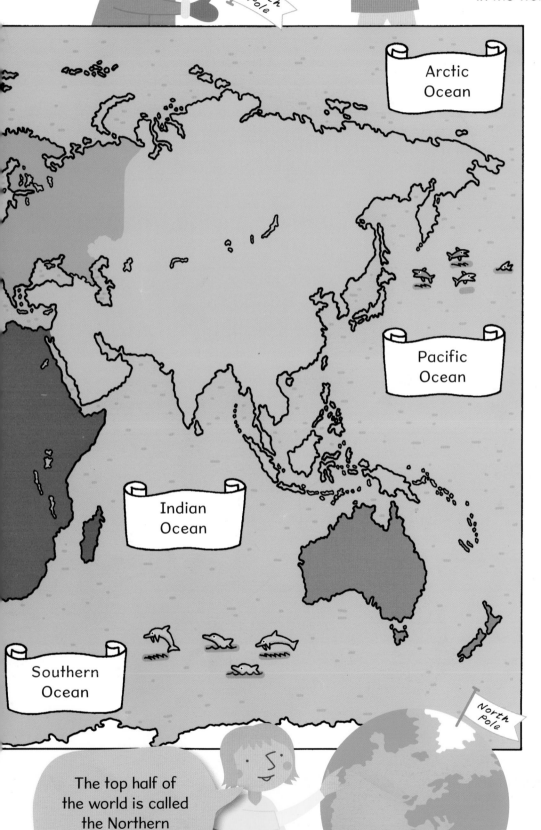

Arctic Ocean

Pacific Ocean

Indian Ocean

Southern Ocean

North Pole

The top half of the world is called the Northern Hemisphere.

MAPS

Maps cannot copy the real size of the places they show. They are drawn to scale, which means that they are shrunk to fit the page.

A small distance on a map stands for a much larger distance in real life. The distance is shown under each map in a scale bar.

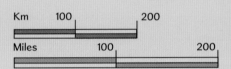

| Km | 100 | | 200 |
| Miles | | 100 | 200 |

For example, this island is 321 km or 200 miles wide.

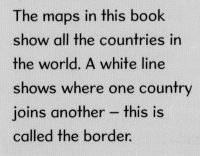

The maps in this book show all the countries in the world. A white line shows where one country joins another — this is called the border.

Ireland

Ireland is an island to the west of the UK. It has 32 counties and four provinces. It is divided between the Republic of Ireland and Northern Ireland, which is part of the United Kingdom. The Republic of Ireland is the largest part. It has 26 counties and a population of over four million people.

Northern Irish flag

Republic of Ireland flag

County Sligo, on the west coast, is famous for its beautiful scenery.

The Irish flag was adopted in 1919. The white centre stripe represents peace.

The Beehive Huts in Dingle have stood for over 4,000 years. People lived in them until around AD 1200.

Atlantic Ocean

Ireland's west coast attracts surfers from all around the world.

DONEGAL

LEITRIM

Sligo

SLIGO

MAYO

Castlebar

Carrick on Shannon

ROSCOMMON

Roscommon

Republic of Ireland

Galway

GALWAY

CLARE

Ennis

TIPPERARY

Limerick

LIMERICK

Tralee

KERRY

CORK

Cork

Kilometres 50 100

Miles 50 100

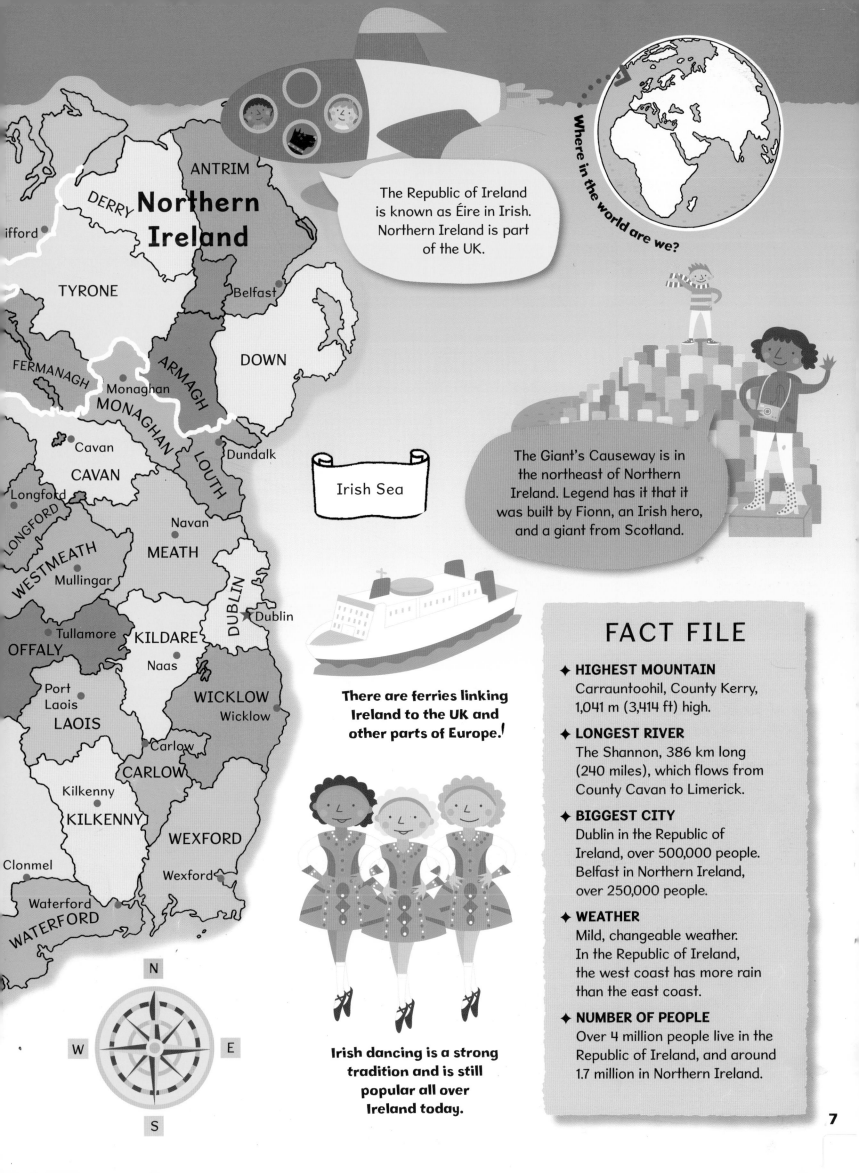

Northern Ireland

ANTRIM

DERRY

ifford

TYRONE

Belfast

FERMANAGH

DOWN

MONAGHAN

ARMAGH

LOUTH

Monaghan

Cavan

CAVAN

Dundalk

Longford

LONGFORD

Navan

WESTMEATH

MEATH

Mullingar

DUBLIN

Dublin

Tullamore

KILDARE

OFFALY

Naas

Port Laois

WICKLOW

LAOIS

Wicklow

Carlow

CARLOW

Kilkenny

KILKENNY

WEXFORD

Clonmel

Wexford

Waterford

WATERFORD

The Republic of Ireland is known as Éire in Irish. Northern Ireland is part of the UK.

Where in the world are we?

The Giant's Causeway is in the northeast of Northern Ireland. Legend has it that it was built by Fionn, an Irish hero, and a giant from Scotland.

Irish Sea

There are ferries linking Ireland to the UK and other parts of Europe.

Irish dancing is a strong tradition and is still popular all over Ireland today.

FACT FILE

◆ **HIGHEST MOUNTAIN**
Carrauntoohil, County Kerry, 1,041 m (3,414 ft) high.

◆ **LONGEST RIVER**
The Shannon, 386 km long (240 miles), which flows from County Cavan to Limerick.

◆ **BIGGEST CITY**
Dublin in the Republic of Ireland, over 500,000 people. Belfast in Northern Ireland, over 250,000 people.

◆ **WEATHER**
Mild, changeable weather. In the Republic of Ireland, the west coast has more rain than the east coast.

◆ **NUMBER OF PEOPLE**
Over 4 million people live in the Republic of Ireland, and around 1.7 million in Northern Ireland.

N
W E
S

The story of Ireland

6,500–7,000 BC
First settlements were built at Mount Sandel, near Coleraine, County Derry.

500 BC
Celtic warriors arrived and conquered Ireland in the next few hundred years.

AD 400
Christianity was introduced. St Patrick arrived around 456 to help convert pagan Gaelic kings to Christianity.

795
Vikings began to raid Ireland for treasure and slaves. They later settled and made Dublin a trading city.

968
Brian Boru, a powerful warlord, recaptured the seat of the Munster Kings from the Vikings. He became first king of all of Ireland in 1002.

1066
Normans invaded England and set their sights on Ireland. Strongbow was sent to help the King of Leinster's army in 1170.

1348
Bubonic plague reached Ireland and killed one third of its population.

1541
Henry VIII declared himself King of Ireland and sent settlers to establish Protestantism.

1594–1603
Hugh O'Neill led a rebellion to stop settlers from England and Scotland from taking Irish lands.

1605
Flight of the Earls. The Earls of Tyrone and Tyrconnell fled the island defeated, as English and Scots settled on Irish land.

1649

Oliver Cromwell conquered Ireland by winning battles at Drogheda and Wexford. Thousands of Catholics were killed, others fled abroad.

1823

Daniel O'Connell set up the Catholic Association. He was called 'the Liberator' for all his efforts to increase Catholic peoples' rights.

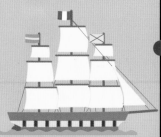

1845–50

The Great Famine. Potato crop failed four years running. A million people starved or died of disease. Another million people fled abroad.

1870

The Home Rule Association was set up. This meant Ireland would have its own parliament.

1916

The Easter Rising. A group of rebels, led by Patrick Pearse and including Michael Collins, seized a number of buildings in Dublin. They aimed to set up an Irish Republic, but were soon defeated.

1919–21

The Irish War of Independence. Irish parliament, Dáil Éireann, held its first meeting. The IRA violently rebelled against British forces.

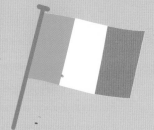

1921

Anglo-Irish Treaty was signed. It divided Ireland into two states.

1937

Constitution of Ireland. The 26 counties were renamed Éire, or 'Ireland' in English, and Éamon de Valera was made first taoiseach.

1985

Anglo-Irish Agreement was signed. Northern Ireland became part of the UK.

1990–97

Mary Robinson was elected as first female president of Ireland.

1998

Good Friday Agreement was signed. Unionist and Nationalist parties agreed to run Northern Ireland together.

2002

Irish currency changed from Punt to Euro.

2007

New-look Northern Ireland Assembly met for the first time.

Things to see

Ireland is packed full of amazing places to visit and incredible things to see. Here is a collection of postcards from all over Ireland. Next to each postcard is a short description telling you all about it.

The Book of Kells (c. AD 800) is a handwritten book of the four gospels, illustrated with colourful pictures. It is kept in Trinity College, Dublin.

Dublin Zoo opened in 1830 and is the third oldest zoo in the world. Situated in Phoenix Park, it houses more than 235 species of wild animals and tropical birds.

Dublin is Ireland's busy capital city. The Custom House is by the River Liffey. It was built in the 18th century and burnt down in 1921, but later restored.

Brú na Bóinne (Boyne Valley) in Co. Meath is famous for its megalithic tombs – Newgrange, Knowth and Dowth – with decorated stones over 10,000 years old.

Ireland is made up of four provinces – Ulster, Munster, Leinster and Connaught. Have you visited all of them?

The Claddagh Village, Co. Galway. Legend has it that a ring symbolising friendship (hands), love (heart) and loyalty (crown) originated here in the 17th century.

Ireland also has islands to visit! The Aran Islands is a group of three islands near **Galway Bay** on the west coast, and **Achill Island** is near **Co. Mayo**.

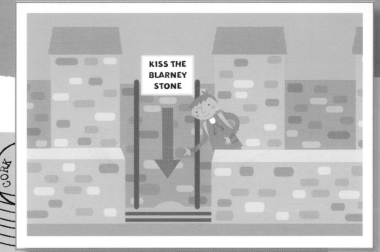

The Blarney Stone, Co. Cork. Visitors can kiss the stone in Blarney Castle by leaning over a 26 m (85 ft) drop! It is believed to grant 'the gift of the gab'.

There was once a great monastery at Glendalough in Co. Wicklow. It was founded by St Kevin and survived until about 1400.

There are many more things to see in and around Ireland. Research other attractions on the internet.

Croagh Patrick, Co. Mayo. Every year on the last Friday of July, thousands of pilgrims climb the **mountain** where Ireland's patron saint is said to have fasted for 40 days.

The Dingle Peninsula in Co. Kerry is on the Southwest coast of Ireland. Fungi the male, bottle-nosed dolphin has been a regular at Dingle Bay since 1984.

The Cliffs of Moher, Co. Clare. They rise 204 m (640 ft) above the sea and stretch for 8 km (5 miles) along the coast.

What people do

The people of Ireland work at various jobs. Since Ireland joined the European Union in 1973, trading and travelling between countries has become easier – especially since the introduction of the Euro as Ireland's currency in 2002.

Design and textiles

There are renowned textile and clothing companies in Belfast, Derry and other towns, as well as many smaller, independent companies.

Aran jumpers

Waterford cut glass

Sport

Gaelic football and hurling are the national sports of Ireland and are organised by the Gaelic Athletic Association (GAA). Rugby, golf and horse-racing are also very popular.

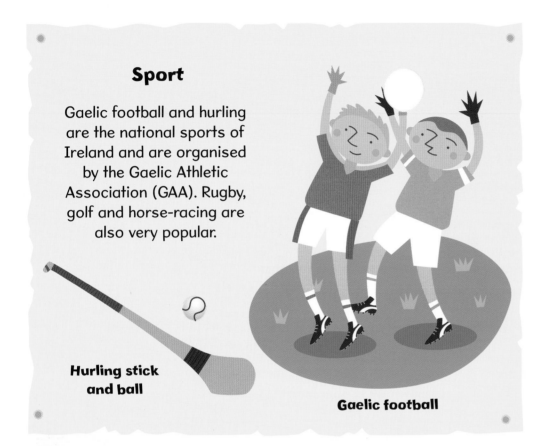

Hurling stick and ball

Gaelic football

Multinationals

Many multinational companies have a strong presence in Ireland, including Dell, Microsoft, Pfizer and Google.

Agriculture

Ireland is a farming country. Many types of animals, poultry and crops such as barley and oats are farmed. Fish are plentiful, too. There are famous Irish brands – Guinness, Tayto and Barry's Tea!

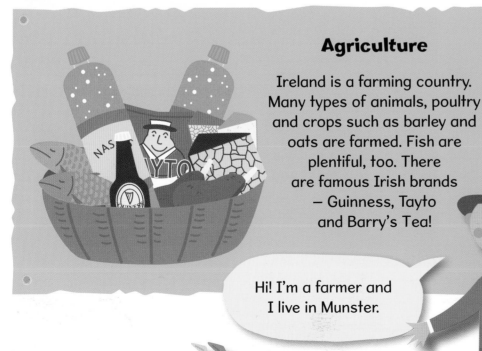

Hi! I'm a farmer and I live in Munster.

Fuel

Ireland uses the natural resource of its bog lands (peatbog and turf bank) to provide heating for homes on a large scale. Briquettes are used in open fires and are smokeless when burned.

Literature

Ireland boasts some of the greatest writers in the world. They include Bram Stoker, Oscar Wilde, James Joyce and Sean O'Casey. Poets include Seamus Heaney, W. B. Yeats and Eavan Boland.

Oscar Wilde

James Joyce

Bram Stoker

Sean O'Casey

Music

Musicians who play traditional music are famous all over the world and use instruments including the fiddle, tin whistle, bodhrán and harp. Popular modern musicians include U2, Van Morrison, The Corrs, Westlife and Damien Rice.

Hi! I'm a musician and I like to play traditional Irish music.

Politics

Ireland has a president, and a taoiseach. The Taoiseach works mainly in Dáil Éireann.

Hi! I'm a banker and I work in Dublin's city centre.

Northern Europe

The countries of Northern Europe together make up an area called Scandinavia. All are members of the EU, except Norway. Only Sweden uses the Euro. The rest use their national currencies. The Vikings came from Northern Europe.

Norway was made into a country by the Viking, Harald Fairhair, in AD 872.

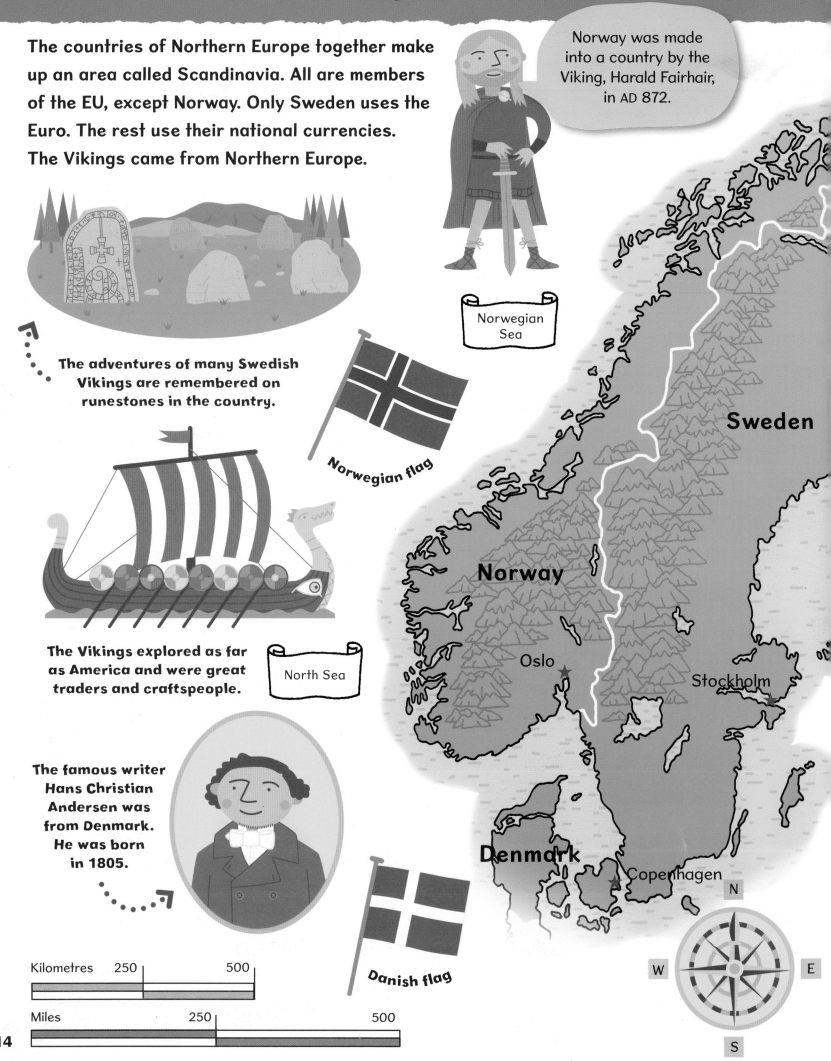

Norwegian Sea

The adventures of many Swedish Vikings are remembered on runestones in the country.

Norwegian flag

The Vikings explored as far as America and were great traders and craftspeople.

North Sea

The famous writer Hans Christian Andersen was from Denmark. He was born in 1805.

Danish flag

Sweden

Norway

Oslo

Stockholm

Denmark

Copenhagen

Kilometres   250   500

Miles   250   500

N

W   E

S

Nokia, the world's largest manufacturer of mobile phones, is based in Finland.

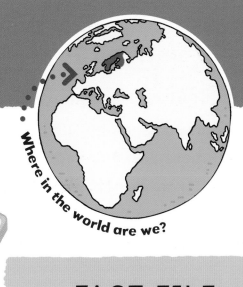

Where in the world are we?

Finnish flag

Finland

Helsinki

Baltic Sea

The Sámi people live in parts of Norway, Sweden, Finland and Russia. Some of them herd reindeer.

Swedish flag

FACT FILE

◆ **HIGHEST MOUNTAIN**
Galdhøpiggen, Norway, 2,469 m (8,100 ft).

◆ **LONGEST RIVER**
Klarälven-Göta, Norway/Sweden, 720 km (447 miles).

◆ **BIGGEST CITY**
Copenhagen, Denmark, about 1.7 million people.

◆ **WEATHER**
Scandinavia has long, cold, dark winters and short, mild summers.

◆ **NUMBER OF PEOPLE**
Finland, about 5.3 million; Norway, about 4.7 million; Sweden, about 9 million; Denmark, about 5.5 million.

Finland is the land of lakes. It has over 50,000! Many freeze over during the long winter months.

Almost half of Norway's income comes from oil and gas wells.

Many Scandinavian families have a sauna. It is a kind of steam bath in a wooden shed.

UK and Central Europe

The United Kingdom (UK) was joined to the continent of Europe until about 200,000 years ago. The landscape of Europe is very varied, from flat farmland to high mountain peaks. Over 230 languages are spoken across the whole of Europe.

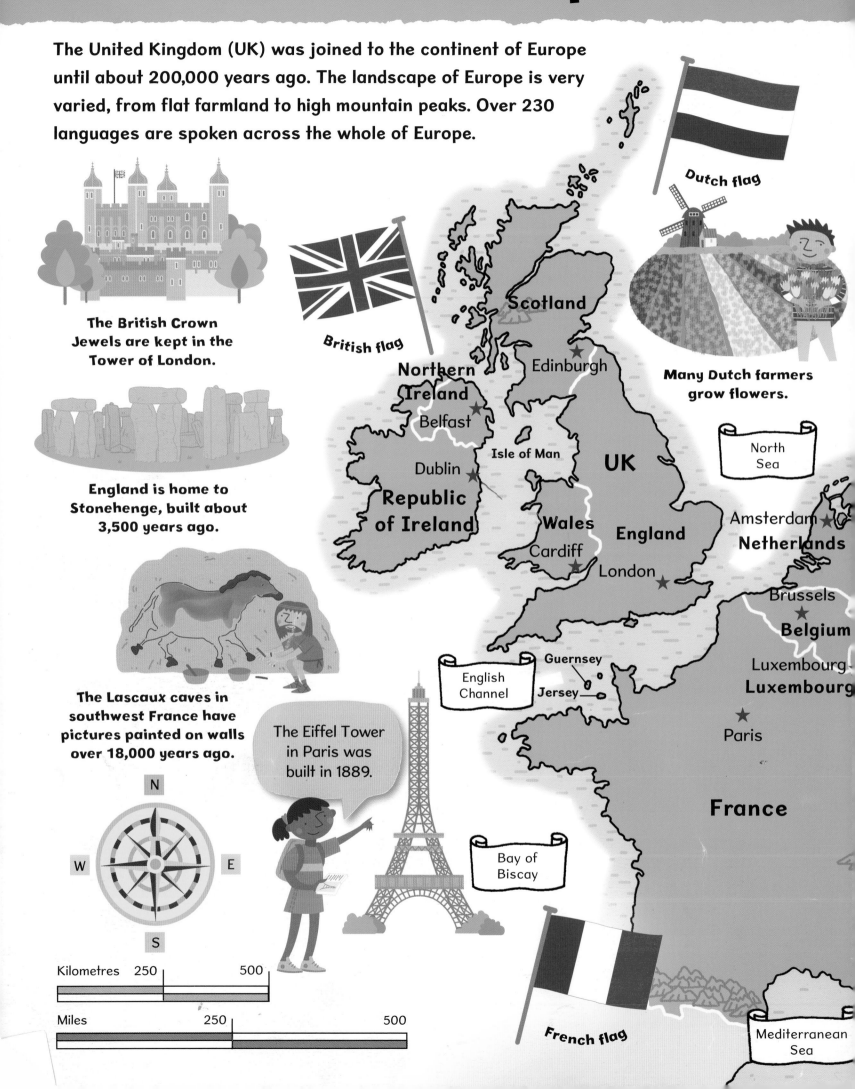

The British Crown Jewels are kept in the Tower of London.

England is home to Stonehenge, built about 3,500 years ago.

The Lascaux caves in southwest France have pictures painted on walls over 18,000 years ago.

The Eiffel Tower in Paris was built in 1889.

Dutch flag

British flag

Many Dutch farmers grow flowers.

Scotland

Edinburgh

Northern Ireland

Belfast

Isle of Man

Dublin

Republic of Ireland

Wales

Cardiff

UK

England

London

North Sea

Amsterdam

Netherlands

Brussels

Belgium

Luxembourg

Luxembourg

Paris

English Channel

Guernsey

Jersey

Bay of Biscay

France

French flag

Mediterranean Sea

N

W — E

S

Kilometres 250 500

Miles 250 500

The Euro is the currency of 16 of the 27 members of the European Union, also known as the EU.

EU flag

Where in the world are we?

Berlin is home to the Brandenburg gate, built in 1788.

Polish flag

Denmark

★ Copenhagen

Berlin ★

Germany

Warsaw ★
Poland

Prague ★

Czech Republic

Slovakia

Vienna ★   ★ Bratislava

Liechtenstein

Austria

Bern
Switzerland

★ Budapest
Hungary

Moldova

★ Chisinau

Romania

Monaco

Wind farms are seen across Europe.

German flag

Bucharest ★

Bulgaria
★ Sofia

Black Sea

FACT FILE

◆ **HIGHEST MOUNTAIN**
Mont Blanc, France, 4810 m (15,784 ft).

◆ **LONGEST RIVER**
The Danube, 2,850 km (1,771 miles).

◆ **BIGGEST CITY**
Paris, France, about 2.2 million people.

◆ **WEATHER**
Most of this part of Europe has mild winters and cool summers. Rain falls all year round. Snow falls on high land in winter.

◆ **NUMBER OF PEOPLE**
France, about 62 million; UK, about 60.9 million; Germany, about 82 million; Netherlands, about 16.7 million; Luxembourg, about 487.5 thousand.

Mediterranean Europe

The countries around the Mediterranean Sea are sunny most of the year. Olives, fruit and vegetables are grown in these countries. Many people travel to the Mediterranean for holidays because of the hot weather, but in parts of Spain and Italy there are high mountains where people go skiing in winter.

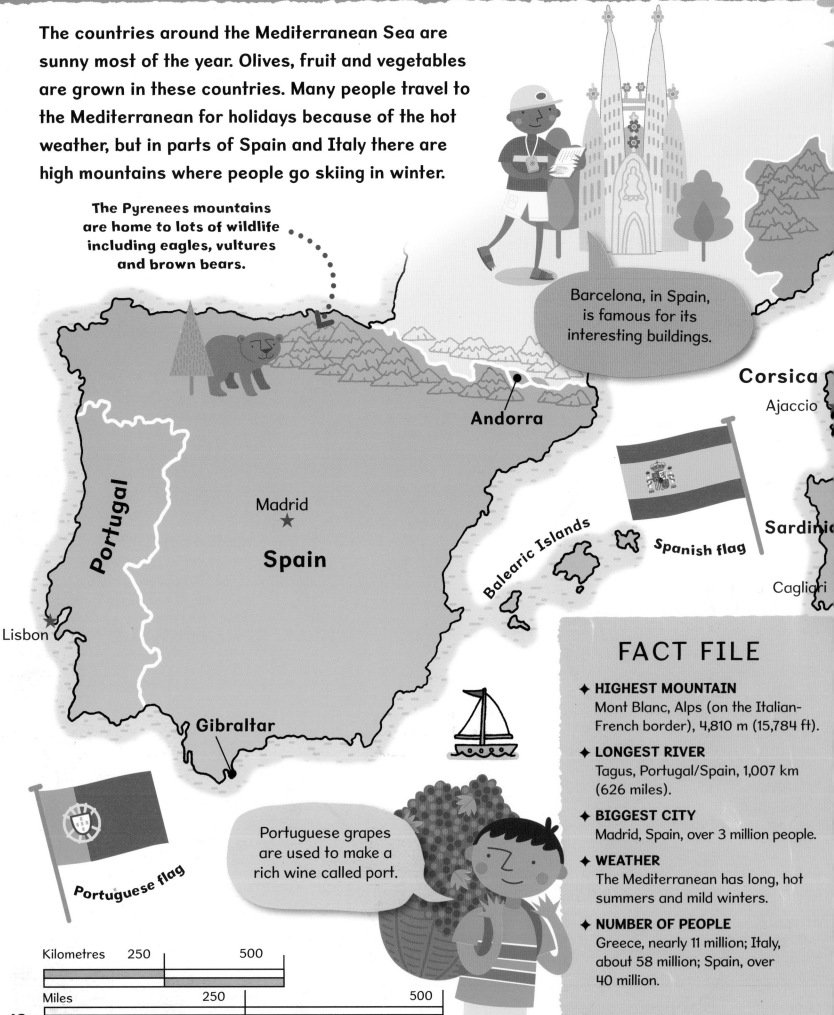

The Pyrenees mountains are home to lots of wildlife including eagles, vultures and brown bears.

Barcelona, in Spain, is famous for its interesting buildings.

Corsica

Ajaccio

Andorra

Portugal

Madrid ★

Spain

Balearic Islands

Spanish flag

Sardinia

Cagliari

Lisbon

Gibraltar

Portuguese flag

Portuguese grapes are used to make a rich wine called port.

FACT FILE

◆ **HIGHEST MOUNTAIN**
Mont Blanc, Alps (on the Italian-French border), 4,810 m (15,784 ft).

◆ **LONGEST RIVER**
Tagus, Portugal/Spain, 1,007 km (626 miles).

◆ **BIGGEST CITY**
Madrid, Spain, over 3 million people.

◆ **WEATHER**
The Mediterranean has long, hot summers and mild winters.

◆ **NUMBER OF PEOPLE**
Greece, nearly 11 million; Italy, about 58 million; Spain, over 40 million.

Kilometres 250 500

Miles 250 500

Venice, in Italy, is built on lots of small islands in the sea. Many of the streets are canals, so people travel around the city in boats.

Where in the world are we?

N
W E
S

Serbia is home to the Obedska Bara Nature Reserve, one of the world's oldest natural wetland areas.

Slovenia
★ Ljubljana

Zagreb
★
Croatia

Belgrade
★

Bosnia & Herzegovina

Serbia

San Marino

★ Sarajevo

Italy

Montenegro
★ Podgorica

Rome
★ Vatican City
△ Mt. Vesuvius

Adriatic Sea

★ Skopje

Tirane
★
Macedonia

Turkey
Istanbul
★

Albania

Milan, in Italy, is world famous for its fashion houses and its catwalks.

Palermo
★
△ Mt. Etna

Greece

Sicily

Greek flag

Mediterranean Sea

The Olympic Games began nearly 3,000 years ago in Ancient Greece.

Athens

There are over 1,400 Greek islands.

★ Valletta
Malta

Crete

The Ancient Greeks and Romans built many fine temples and buildings. Today tourists go to see the ruins.

Italian flag

Sicily is home to Mount Etna, a live volcano. It is about 2½ times taller than Mount Vesuvius, near Rome.

Eastern Europe and Russia

Russia is the biggest country in the world. It stretches from Europe to the Far East and takes up about one eighth of Earth's land surface.

The European part of Russia in the West is divided from the Eastern part by the Ural Mountains.

Russian Yuri Gagarin was the first person to blast into space, aboard Vostok 1 in 1961.

Arctic Ocean

Barents Sea

Kara Sea

The Brown Bear is the national symbol of Russia. It is now endangered.

Russia

Ural Mountains

Estonia
Tallinn
Riga
Lithuania
Vilnius
Minsk
Moscow
Latvia
Belarus
Astana
Kiev
Ukraine
Kazakhstan
There are rich supplies of oil, gas and coal under the ground.
Bishkek
Georgia
Tbilisi
Baku
Uzbekistan
Tashkent
Kyrgyzstan
Yerevan
Armenia
Azerbaijan
Turkmenistan
Dushanbe
Ashgabat
Tajikistan

MOCKBA

Preevyet! (Hello!)
I live in Moscow, Russia.
I speak Russian and English
and I write in Russian Cyrillic.

Russian flag

FACT FILE

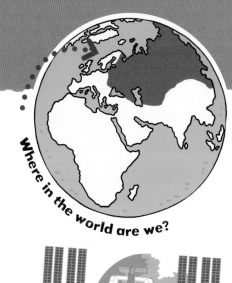

◆ **HIGHEST MOUNTAIN**
Ismoil Somoni Peak
(formerly Communism Peak),
7,495 m (24,590 ft).

◆ **LONGEST RIVER**
The Ob-Irtysh, 5,410 km
(3,362 miles).

◆ **BIGGEST CITY**
Moscow, about 10.5 million people.

◆ **WEATHER**
In the north there is Arctic ice.
In the south there is a burning
desert. Most places inland have
hot summers and cold winters.

◆ **NUMBER OF PEOPLE**
Russia, about 140 million.

Laptev
Sea

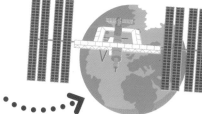

Russia launched and
helped to build the
International Space
Station.

East
Siberian Sea

Chukchi
Sea

Russia

Moscow is the
capital of Russia.
It has amazing
onion-shaped
domes.

Sea of
Okhotsk

N

W   E

S

Russian dancers are
famous all over the world.

Wheat is the most important
Russian crop.

Kilometres	1000

Miles	1000

North America

North America is the third largest continent. It contains Canada, the United States of America, Mexico and around 40 smaller nations. In less than 400 years since its discovery by Europeans, it has become one of the most powerful industrial areas in the world.

Inuit and Canadian Indians were the first people to live in Canada.

Alaska

Juneau

Canada

Ice hockey is the most popular sport in Canada. The first competition was played in Montreal in 1875.

USA flag

National Parks in the USA help to preserve some wilderness.

The Hollywood sign has been in the hills above Los Angeles since 1923.

North Pacific Ocean

United States

The Aztecs and Maya were famous ancient civilisations of Mexico.

Hawaii

Hawaii is the 50th state of America. It is almost 2,000 miles (3,200 km) from the mainland!

Mexico

Kilometres 1000

Miles 1000

100

Mexican flag

Mexico City

Clipperton Island

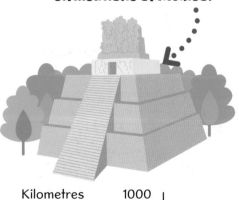

Canadian flag

The Statue of Liberty, New York, was given to America by France in 1886, to celebrate 100 years of independence.

Niagara Falls are famous waterfalls on the border between the USA and Canada.

Where in the world are we?

FACT FILE

◆ **HIGHEST MOUNTAIN**
Mount McKinley, Alaska, 6,198 m (20,334 ft).

◆ **LONGEST RIVER**
Mississippi-Missouri 5,970 km (3,709 miles).

◆ **BIGGEST CITY**
Mexico City, about 8.8 million.

◆ **WEATHER**
Canada and Alaska are the coldest parts of North America. It is hot in central America and the West Indies.

◆ **NUMBER OF PEOPLE**
Canada, about 33.5 million; USA, about 308 million; Mexico, about 111 million; Costa Rica, about 4.3 million; Panama, about 3.4 million.

Ottawa

Niagara Falls

Washington DC

The West Indian islands were discovered in 1492 by Christopher Columbus.

Bermuda

North Atlantic Ocean

The White House in Washington has been the home of the President of the United States of America since 1801.

The Bahamas

Turks and Caicos Islands

Virgin Islands

Anguilla

Antigua & Barbuda

Guadeloupe

Dominica

Haiti

Cuba

Gulf of Mexico

Cayman Islands

Puerto Rico

St Kitts and Nevis

Martinique

St Lucia

Barbados

Grenada

Jamaica

Dominican Republic

St Vincent and the Grenadines

Trinidad & Tobago

Belize

Honduras

Belmopan

uatemala

atemala

an Salvador

Tegucigalpa

Nicaragua

Managua

Panama

San Jose

Panama

Costa Rica

Salvador

Netherland Antilles

Hurricanes cause a lot of damage each year in the West Indies.

N

W   E

S

23

South America

South America is the fourth largest continent, after North America. It was named after Amerigo Vespuci, who suggested it was a new land unknown to Europeans, in 1507. The continent is very varied, from cold deserts to steaming rainforests.

Colombian flag

Aruba

Netherland Antilles

Caracas

Venezuela

★ Bogotá

Colombia

★ Quito

Ecuador

Peru

Lima ★

Bolivia

La Paz ★

South Pacific Ocean

Chile

★ Santiago

Argentine

Tango dancing is popular, especially in Argentina.

Peruvian flag

Machu Picchu, in Peru, was built by Pachacuti Inca Yupanqui, an Incan ruler about 500 years ago.

Giant anteaters eat ants, with a long sticky tongue.

Venezuelan flag

Many tribes lived in South America before the Europeans and others arrived. The Mapuche lived in Chile.

Some South Americans work on horseback and are called gauchos.

Chilean flag

N
W   E
S

Kilometres   50   100

Miles   50   100

There are thought to be some tribes in the Amazon rainforest who have never made contact with the outside world.

Where in the world are we?

Georgetown
Paramaribo
French Guiana
Cayenne
Suriname
uyana

Poison dart frogs live in the rainforests. Some are used to make poison arrows.

The Amazon rainforest

Brazil

Brasilia ★

The Amazon rainforest is the world's largest. It covers 5.5 million square kilometres.

Llamas are used to carry things, and for their meat and fur.

araguay
Asunción

Uruguay

South Atlantic Ocean

Montevideo
Buenos Aires

Brazilian flag

The city of São Paulo, in Brazil, has the largest population in South America.

FACT FILE

◆ **HIGHEST MOUNTAIN**
Cerro Aconcagua, Argentina, 6,960 m, (22,834 ft).

◆ **LONGEST RIVER**
The Amazon, which runs through Peru, Columbia and Brazil, 6,516 km (4,049 miles).

◆ **BIGGEST CITY**
São Paulo, about 11 million people.

◆ **WEATHER**
It is mainly hot and wet. However, the weather can vary greatly.

◆ **NUMBER OF PEOPLE**
Chile, about 17 million; Argentina, about 40.1 million; Brazil, nearly 200 million.

Argentinian flag

Argentinian school children wear white coats for their school uniform.

Stanley

Falkland Islands

South Georgia and South Sandwich Islands

Christ the Redeemer is a 38 m (125 ft) tall statue in Rio de Janeiro, Brazil.

Africa

Africa is the second largest continent in the world. About one billion people live there in 61 different territories or 53 countries. Africa has many kinds of landscape, from the Sahara desert to the rainforests of the central area. It is thought to be the origin of the human population about 200,000 years ago.

There are lots of different cultures and tribes in Africa and about 2,000 languages spoken!

Moroccan flag

Nigerian flag

The Venetia mine is the largest in South Africa. Rocks are dug up and crushed to find diamonds.

South African flag

North Atlantic Ocean

South Atlantic Ocean

St Helena

Western Sahara

El Aaiun

Morocco

Rabat

Algiers

Tunis

Tunisia

Algeria

Mauritania

Nouakchott

Cape Verde

Senegal

Dakar

Gambia

Banjul

Bissau

Guinea-Bissau

Guinea

Conakry

Freetown

Sierra Leone

Monrovia

Liberia

Yamoussoukro

Mali

Bamako

Niamey

Burkina Faso

Bagré

Côte d'Ivoire

Ghana

Accra

Togo

Benin

Lomé

Porto Novo

Abuja

Niger

Nigeria

Malabo

Equatorial Guinea

Saotome and Principe

Libraville

Gabon

Many giraffes grow to 8 m (26 ft) high in southern Africa. Acacia trees are their favourite food.

N

W

E

S

The Victoria Falls, between Zambia and Zimbabwe, is the world's largest sheet of falling water.

Kilometres 1000

Miles 1000

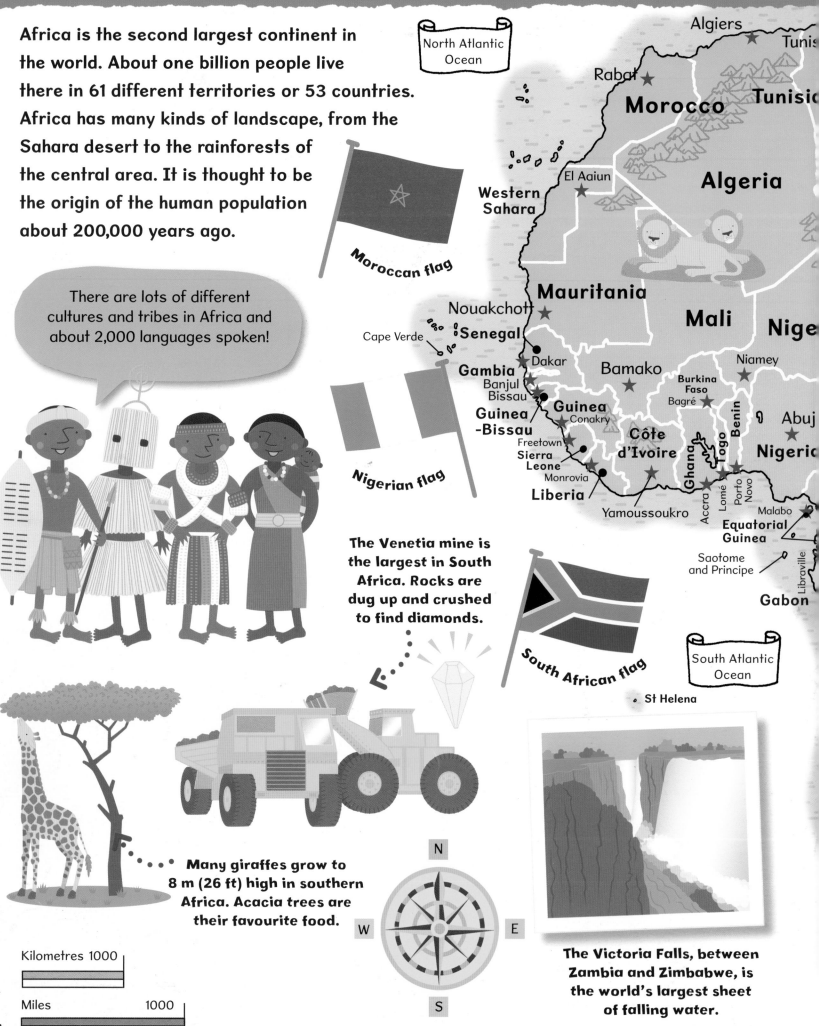

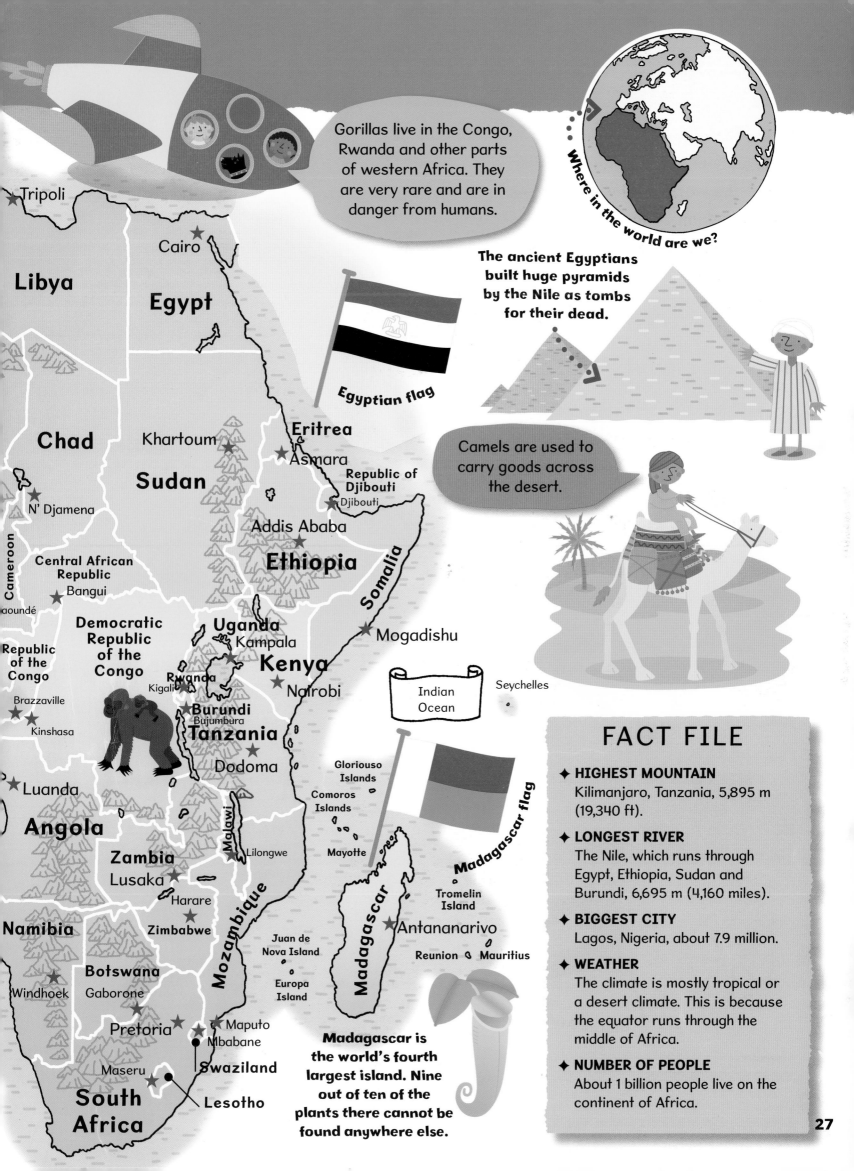

Gorillas live in the Congo, Rwanda and other parts of western Africa. They are very rare and are in danger from humans.

Where in the world are we?

The ancient Egyptians built huge pyramids by the Nile as tombs for their dead.

Egyptian flag

Camels are used to carry goods across the desert.

Tripoli

Libya

Cairo

Egypt

Chad

Khartoum

Sudan

N' Djamena

Cameroon

Central African Republic

Bangui

aoundé

Eritrea

Asmara

Republic of Djibouti

Djibouti

Addis Ababa

Ethiopia

Somalia

Democratic Republic of the Congo

Republic of the Congo

Brazzaville

Kinshasa

Uganda

Kampala

Rwanda

Kigali

Burundi

Bujumbura

Tanzania

Dodoma

Kenya

Nairobi

Mogadishu

Indian Ocean

Seychelles

Luanda

Angola

Malawi

Lilongwe

Glorious Islands

Comoros Islands

Mayotte

Madagascar flag

Zambia

Lusaka

Harare

Zimbabwe

Madagascar

Antananarivo

Tromelin Island

Reunion   Mauritius

Namibia

Windhoek

Botswana

Gaborone

Mozambique

Juan de Nova Island

Europa Island

Pretoria

Maputo

Mbabane

Maseru

Swaziland

Lesotho

South Africa

Madagascar is the world's fourth largest island. Nine out of ten of the plants there cannot be found anywhere else.

FACT FILE

◆ **HIGHEST MOUNTAIN**
Kilimanjaro, Tanzania, 5,895 m (19,340 ft).

◆ **LONGEST RIVER**
The Nile, which runs through Egypt, Ethiopia, Sudan and Burundi, 6,695 m (4,160 miles).

◆ **BIGGEST CITY**
Lagos, Nigeria, about 7.9 million.

◆ **WEATHER**
The climate is mostly tropical or a desert climate. This is because the equator runs through the middle of Africa.

◆ **NUMBER OF PEOPLE**
About 1 billion people live on the continent of Africa.

The Middle East

Most of the Middle East is either mountainous or hot, sandy desert. It supplies over half of the world's oil. The oil is pumped up to the surface and then sold to other countries for use as petrol and other fuels.

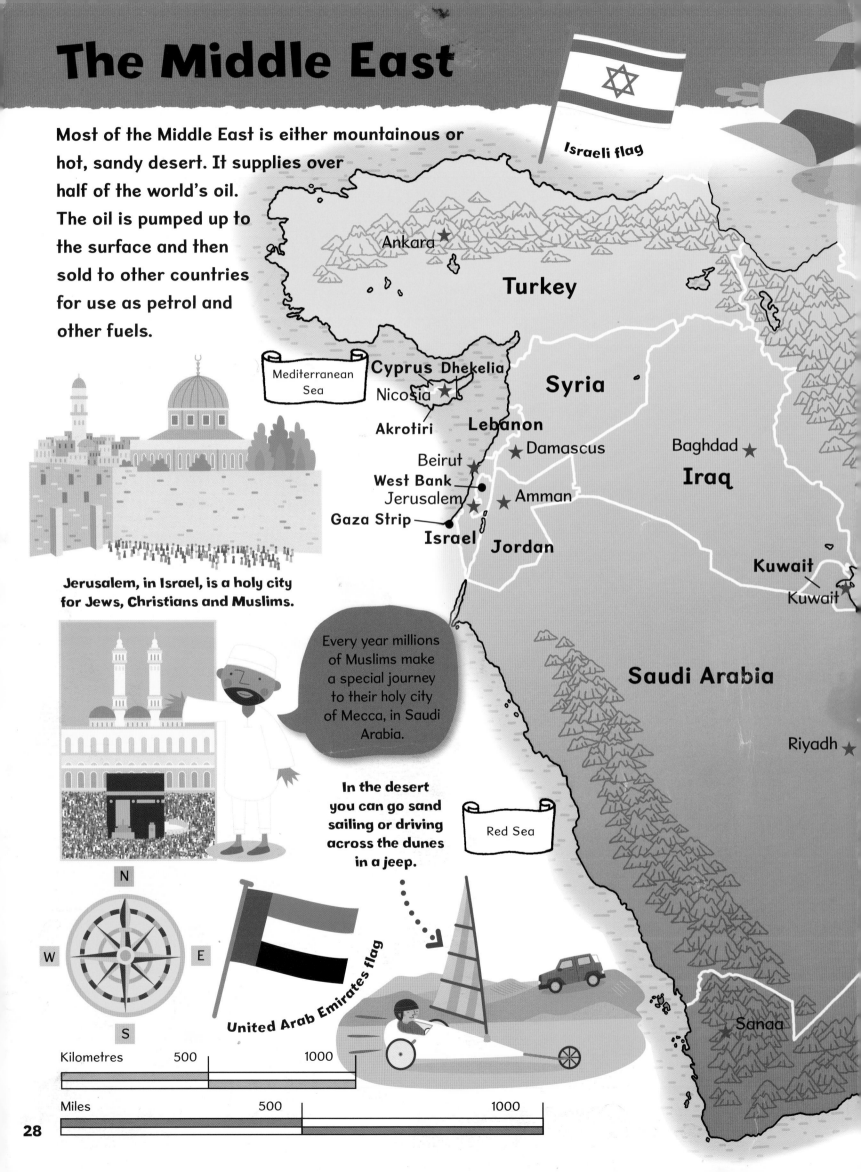

Israeli flag

Jerusalem, in Israel, is a holy city for Jews, Christians and Muslims.

Every year millions of Muslims make a special journey to their holy city of Mecca, in Saudi Arabia.

In the desert you can go sand sailing or driving across the dunes in a jeep.

United Arab Emirates flag

Turkey

Ankara

Mediterranean Sea

Cyprus   Dhekelia

Nicosia

Akrotiri

Lebanon

Beirut

West Bank

Jerusalem

Gaza Strip

Israel

Syria

Damascus

Amman

Jordan

Baghdad

Iraq

Kuwait

Kuwait

Saudi Arabia

Red Sea

Riyadh

Sanaa

N
W   E
S

Kilometres   500   1000

Miles   500   1000

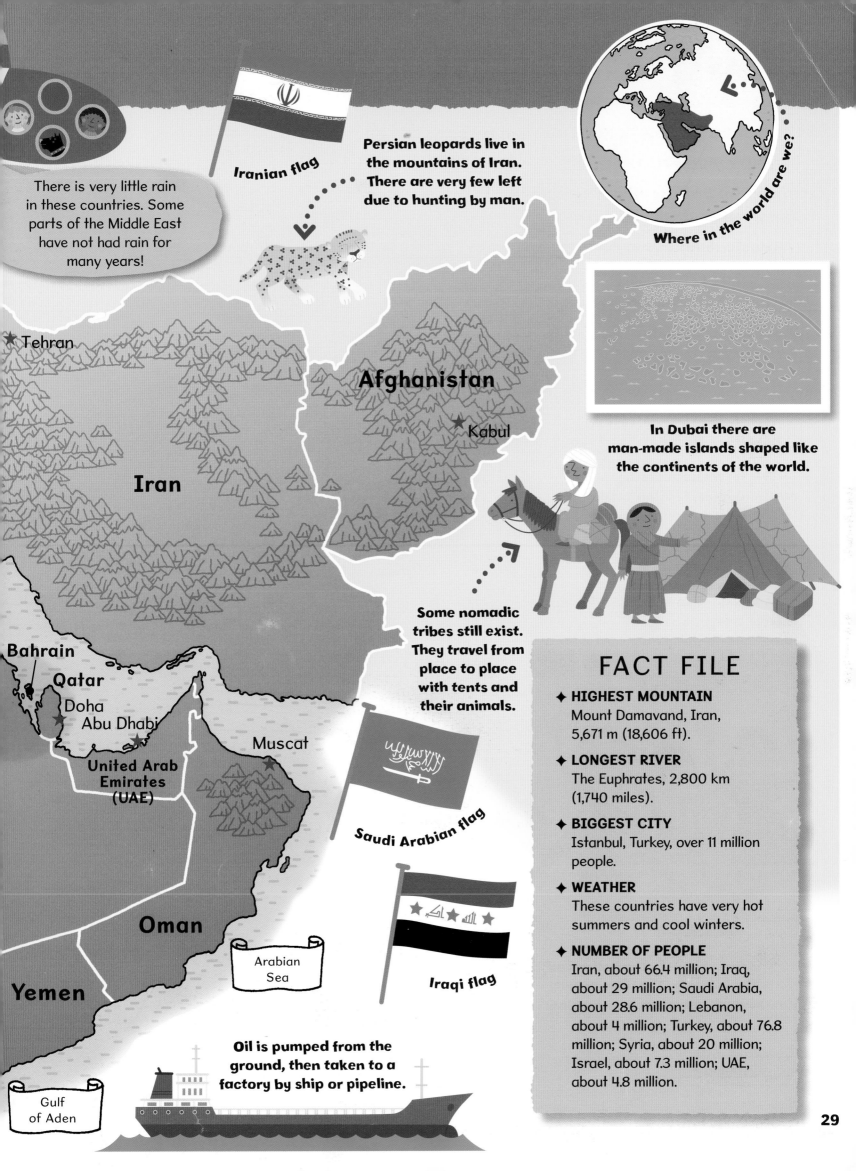

There is very little rain in these countries. Some parts of the Middle East have not had rain for many years!

Iranian flag

Persian leopards live in the mountains of Iran. There are very few left due to hunting by man.

Where in the world are we?

In Dubai there are man-made islands shaped like the continents of the world.

★ Tehran

Iran

Afghanistan

★ Kabul

Bahrain

Qatar

Doha

Abu Dhabi

United Arab Emirates (UAE)

Muscat

Some nomadic tribes still exist. They travel from place to place with tents and their animals.

Saudi Arabian flag

Oman

Arabian Sea

Iraqi flag

Yemen

Oil is pumped from the ground, then taken to a factory by ship or pipeline.

Gulf of Aden

FACT FILE

◆ **HIGHEST MOUNTAIN**
Mount Damavand, Iran, 5,671 m (18,606 ft).

◆ **LONGEST RIVER**
The Euphrates, 2,800 km (1,740 miles).

◆ **BIGGEST CITY**
Istanbul, Turkey, over 11 million people.

◆ **WEATHER**
These countries have very hot summers and cool winters.

◆ **NUMBER OF PEOPLE**
Iran, about 66.4 million; Iraq, about 29 million; Saudi Arabia, about 28.6 million; Lebanon, about 4 million; Turkey, about 76.8 million; Syria, about 20 million; Israel, about 7.3 million; UAE, about 4.8 million.

South Asia

Much of South Asia is farmland, and relies on heavy monsoon rains between June and October for crops to grow. The Himalayas has some of the highest mountains in the world, dividing South Asia from China.

Pakistani flag

Islamabad

Pakistan

New Delhi

The shape of an Asian elephant's ear is the same as the outline of India!

India

The Taj Mahal, near Agra in northern India, is often called the world's most beautiful building.

The Khyber railway runs from Peshwar in Pakistan to the Afghan border. Its carriages are pulled by one steam train and pushed by another.

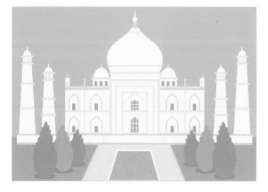

Arabian Sea

More tea is grown in India than anywhere else in the world.

India is home to the Bollywood film industry. The films usually have lots of music and dancing.

British Indian Ocean Territory

N

W E

S

Kilometres 500

Miles 500

Maldives

Indian Ocean

30

Crops need the monsoon rains, but the storms sometimes cause terrible floods, which can destroy whole villages.

Bangladeshi flag

Where in the world are we?

Indian flag

The Himalayan Mountains are too icy to cross in the winter.

Nepal

Kathmandu

Bhutan

Thimphu

Dhaka

Bangladesh

Cows are sacred in India and are allowed to graze where they like.

Cotton plants produce threads that are made into fabric. It can be painted and dyed to be made into clothes, such as sarees.

Cotton plant

Bay of Bengal

Sri Lankan flag

Horses, yaks and even sheep are still used to carry goods across the Himalayas.

Sri Lanka

Colombo

FACT FILE

◆ **HIGHEST MOUNTAIN**
Mount Everest, 8,850 m (29,035 ft).

◆ **LONGEST RIVER** Indus, 3,180 km (1,976 miles).

◆ **BIGGEST CITY**
Mumbai, India, nearly 14 million people.

◆ **WEATHER**
It is very cold in the mountain areas, but hot most of the year elsewhere.

◆ **NUMBER OF PEOPLE**
India, about 1.2 billion; Pakistan, about 76.2 million; Sri Lanka, about 21.3 million; Bangladesh, about 156 million.

Southeast Asia and the Pacific Islands is an area that curves from Myanmur through a chain of islands towards Australia. There are over 7,000 islands in the Philippines alone. It is warm all year round, but the monsoon winds bring heavy rains that damage the houses.

Some villages are built on rivers and the houses have to be built on stilts.

Vietnam flag

Ha Long Bay in Vietnam has many tiny islands, which rise from the sea. Each is named after the shape it resembles.

Singapore flag

The water surrounding the islands are famous for scuba diving because of the beautiful coral reefs.

Many mountains are volcanoes – a hole where molten rock gushes out from the earth.

Myanmar (Burma)

Hanoi ★

Naypyida ★

Vientiane ★

Thailand

Laos

Bangkok ★

Cambodia

Vietnam

Phnom Penh ★

Andaman Sea

South China Sea

Kuala Lumpar ★

Malaysian flag

Malaysia

Singapore

Banda Sea

Indonesia

Jakarta ★

N

W   E

S

Cocos (Keeling) Islands

Christmas Island

Kilometres   500   1000

Miles   500   1000

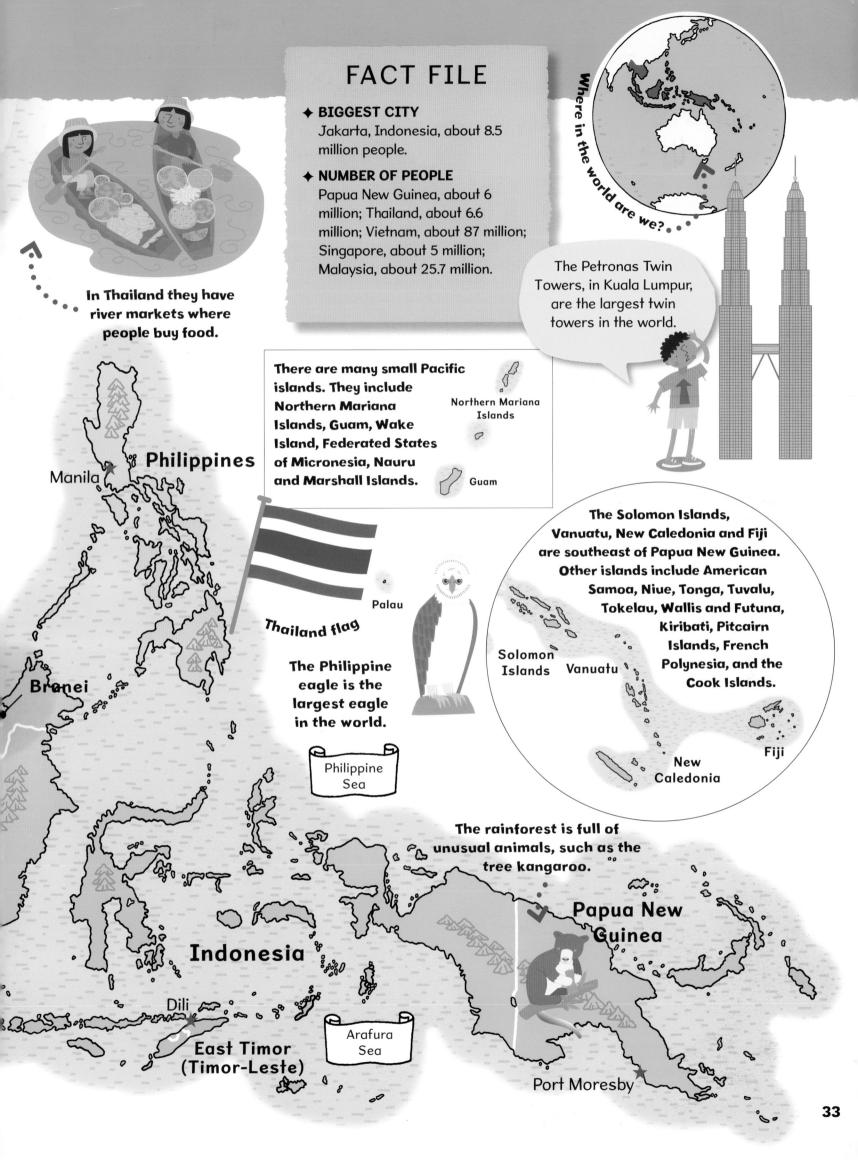

In Thailand they have river markets where people buy food.

FACT FILE

◆ **BIGGEST CITY**
Jakarta, Indonesia, about 8.5 million people.

◆ **NUMBER OF PEOPLE**
Papua New Guinea, about 6 million; Thailand, about 6.6 million; Vietnam, about 87 million; Singapore, about 5 million; Malaysia, about 25.7 million.

Where in the world are we?

The Petronas Twin Towers, in Kuala Lumpur, are the largest twin towers in the world.

There are many small Pacific islands. They include Northern Mariana Islands, Guam, Wake Island, Federated States of Micronesia, Nauru and Marshall Islands.

Northern Mariana Islands

Guam

The Solomon Islands, Vanuatu, New Caledonia and Fiji are southeast of Papua New Guinea. Other islands include American Samoa, Niue, Tonga, Tuvalu, Tokelau, Wallis and Futuna, Kiribati, Pitcairn Islands, French Polynesia, and the Cook Islands.

Solomon Islands

Vanuatu

New Caledonia

Fiji

Philippines

Manila

Palau

Thailand flag

The Philippine eagle is the largest eagle in the world.

Philippine Sea

Brunei

The rainforest is full of unusual animals, such as the tree kangaroo.

Papua New Guinea

Indonesia

Dili

Arafura Sea

East Timor (Timor-Leste)

Port Moresby

East Asia

China is the fourth largest country in the world but has the largest number of people. Japan is much smaller, about the same size as Britain, and is one of the richest countries in Asia.

Horses are an important part of Mongol culture, dating back thousands of years.

Mongolian flag

Mongolia

★ Ulaanbaatar

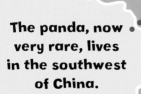

Chinese flag

China

The panda, now very rare, lives in the southwest of China.

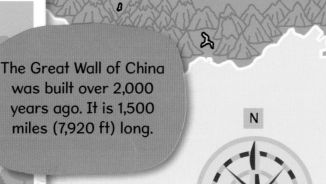

The Great Wall of China was built over 2,000 years ago. It is 1,500 miles (7,920 ft) long.

N

W   E

S

China has many factories which manufacture products for the world mass market.

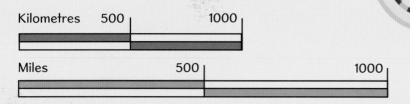

Kilometres   500   1000

Miles   500   1000

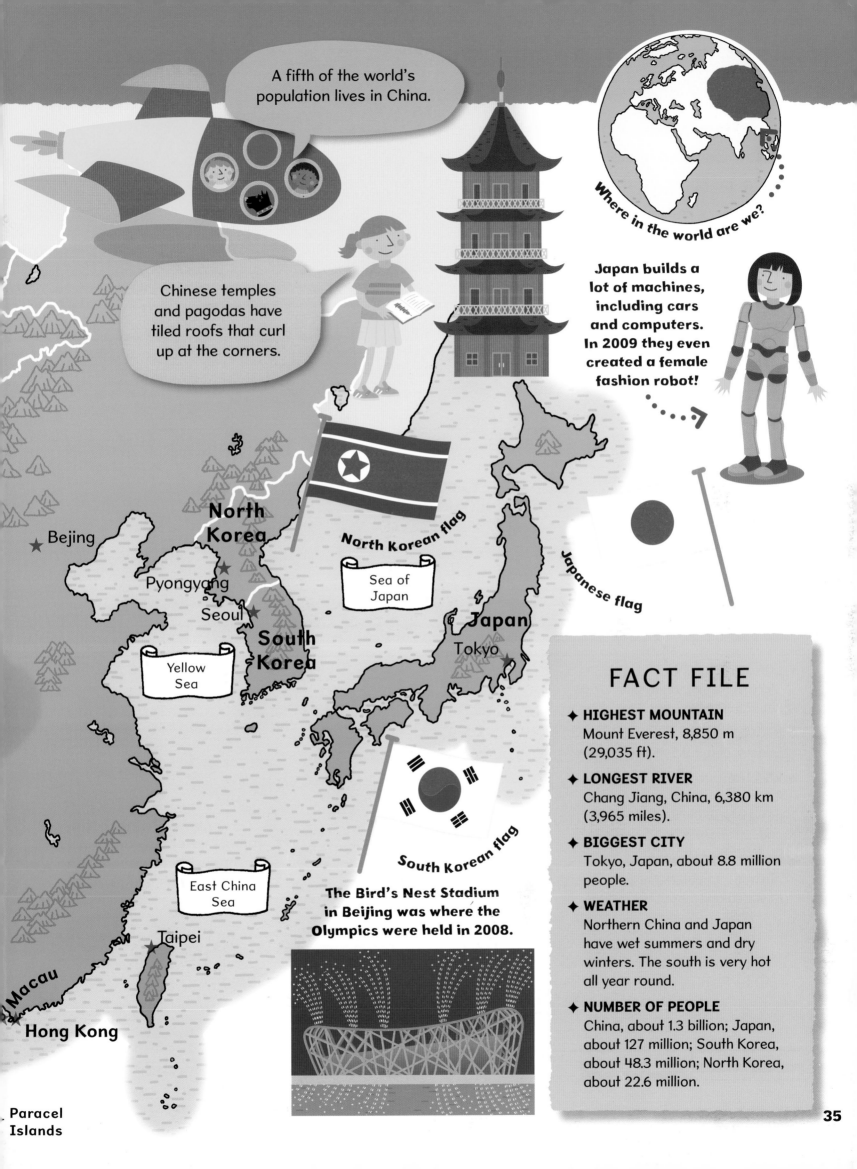

A fifth of the world's population lives in China.

Chinese temples and pagodas have tiled roofs that curl up at the corners.

Where in the world are we?

Japan builds a lot of machines, including cars and computers. In 2009 they even created a female fashion robot!

North Korea

North Korean flag

Bejing

Pyongyang

Seoul

South Korea

Yellow Sea

Sea of Japan

Japan

Tokyo

Japanese flag

South Korean flag

East China Sea

Macau

Taipei

The Bird's Nest Stadium in Beijing was where the Olympics were held in 2008.

Hong Kong

FACT FILE

◆ **HIGHEST MOUNTAIN**
Mount Everest, 8,850 m (29,035 ft).

◆ **LONGEST RIVER**
Chang Jiang, China, 6,380 km (3,965 miles).

◆ **BIGGEST CITY**
Tokyo, Japan, about 8.8 million people.

◆ **WEATHER**
Northern China and Japan have wet summers and dry winters. The south is very hot all year round.

◆ **NUMBER OF PEOPLE**
China, about 1.3 billion; Japan, about 127 million; South Korea, about 48.3 million; North Korea, about 22.6 million.

Paracel Islands

35

Australia and New Zealand

The continent which includes Australia and New Zealand is called Australasia. It is the smallest continent in the world. It lies in the southern Pacific Ocean, on the opposite side of the world from Europe. Most of Australia is flat and dry. New Zealand is more hilly and green.

Surfing is a popular sport in Australia.

Aboriginal art is made up of dots and lines. They believe that their paintings hold the spirits of the animals they draw.

Arafura Sea

Cartier Island

Ashmore Island

Timor Sea

FACT FILE

✦ **HIGHEST MOUNTAIN**
Mount Cook (Aoraki), New Zealand, 3,754 m (12,316 ft).

✦ **LONGEST RIVER**
Murray-Darling, Australia, 3,750 km (2,330 miles).

✦ **BIGGEST CITY**
Sydney, about 4.5 million people.

✦ **WEATHER**
Parts of Australia are very hot desert. New Zealand is cooler and has more rain.

✦ **NUMBER OF PEOPLE**
Australia, about 21.3 million; New Zealand, about 4.3 million.

Australia

Kangaroos, wombats and koalas belong to the Marsupial family. These animals carry their babies in pouches.

N
W   E
S

Kilometres 500   1000

Miles   500   1000

Uluru is a huge sandstone rock in central Australia. At sunset the rock appears to change colour from red to purple.

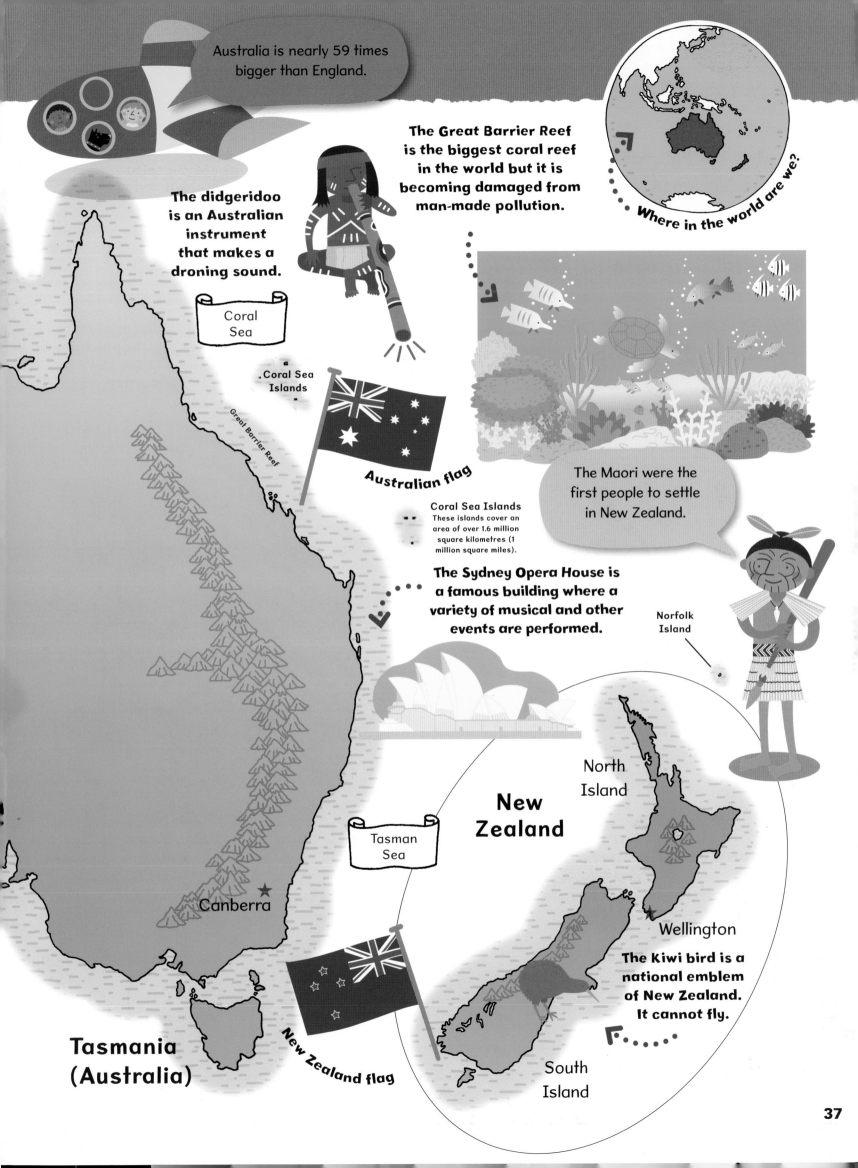

Australia is nearly 59 times bigger than England.

The Great Barrier Reef is the biggest coral reef in the world but it is becoming damaged from man-made pollution.

Where in the world are we?

The didgeridoo is an Australian instrument that makes a droning sound.

Coral Sea

.Coral Sea Islands

Great Barrier Reef

Australian flag

Coral Sea Islands
These islands cover an area of over 1.6 million square kilometres (1 million square miles).

The Maori were the first people to settle in New Zealand.

The Sydney Opera House is a famous building where a variety of musical and other events are performed.

Norfolk Island

North Island

New Zealand

Tasman Sea

Wellington

The Kiwi bird is a national emblem of New Zealand. It cannot fly.

Canberra

Tasmania (Australia)

New Zealand flag

South Island

The Arctic

The Arctic is the area around the North Pole.
It is frozen ocean surrounded by parts of Canada,
Greenland, Alaska, Russia, Iceland, Norway, Sweden
and Finland. Due to global warming the ice around
the North Pole is shrinking.

Inuit people live in the Arctic parts of Canada, Alaska and Greenland.

Aurora Borealis (or northern lights) are mysterious lights that appear in the sky near the North Pole.

The Arctic Circle

Russia

Reindeer can be found in the Arctic.

Arctic

Canada

Greenland

Svalbard

Greenland flag

Arctic Ocean

Iceland

Icelandic flag

Faroe Islands

Kilometres 800   1600

Miles   800   1600

FACT FILE

◆ **HIGHEST MOUNTAIN**
Vinson Massif, Antarctica,
489 m (16,066 ft).
Gunnbjornsfjeld, Arctic,
3,693 m (12,116 ft).

◆ **WEATHER**
Winter and summer last six
months each. In winter it is dark
all day and in summer it is light
all day. When it is winter at one
pole it is summer at the other.

◆ **NUMBER OF PEOPLE**
The Antarctic has no record of
native people, whereas the Arctic
has about four million people.

The Antarctic

The Antarctic is ice-covered land around the South Pole. The ice is thousands of metres thick in some places. There are many high mountains and volcanoes, some even under the ice.

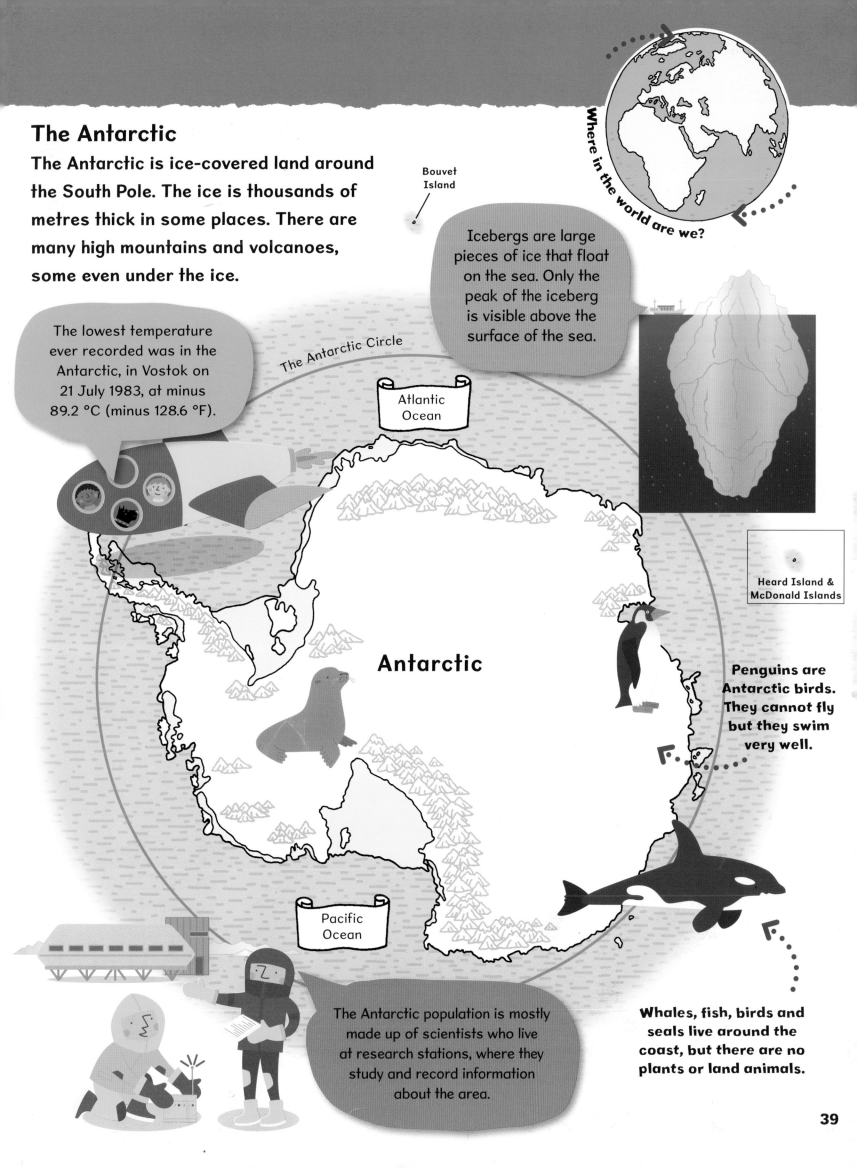

Where in the world are we?

Bouvet Island

Icebergs are large pieces of ice that float on the sea. Only the peak of the iceberg is visible above the surface of the sea.

The lowest temperature ever recorded was in the Antarctic, in Vostok on 21 July 1983, at minus 89.2 °C (minus 128.6 °F).

The Antarctic Circle

Atlantic Ocean

Heard Island & McDonald Islands

Antarctic

Penguins are Antarctic birds. They cannot fly but they swim very well.

Pacific Ocean

The Antarctic population is mostly made up of scientists who live at research stations, where they study and record information about the area.

Whales, fish, birds and seals live around the coast, but there are no plants or land animals.

Index

This book was conceived, edited and designed for Gill & Macmillan Ltd by Tony Potter Publishing Ltd
www.tonypotter.com

Map on page 6–7 based on reference supplied by Oxford Cartographers.

Gill & Macmillan Ltd
Hume Avenue, Park West,
Dublin 12
with associated companies throughout the world
www.gillmacmillan.ie

ISBN: 978-0-7171-4719-9